LUFTWAFFE AT WAR

Luftwaffe Aces of the Western Front

D1518941

Wilhelm-Ferdinand Galland, the younger brother of Adolf Galland, was one of the most gifted fighter aces of the Jagdwaffe, in spite of starting his pilot career as late as 1940, after transferring from Flak to a flying school. He entered frontline service in June 1941, in *JG 26*, the third of three brothers to serve in this unit. His first air victory came one month after that, and at the end of 1942 he was already famous as one of the best fighter pilots in the West. There were 21 kills to his credit by then, and he commanded *5 Staffel* well. Early in 1943 he was promoted to the command of *II Gruppe*, and problems developed because he initially found that the *Gruppe* was too big a unit for him. In May 1943 'Wutz' – as his friends called him – received the *Ritterkreuz* for 41 kills, and before his death on 17 August 1943 he increased his score to 55 victories, achieved in only 186 missions.

LUFTWAFFE AT WAR

Luftwaffe Aces of the Western Front

Robert Michulec

Greenhill Books
LONDON

Stackpole Books
PENNSYLVANIA

Greenhill Books

Luftwaffe Aces of the Western Front first published 2002
by Greenhill Books, Lionel Leventhal Limited, Park
House, 1 Russell Gardens, London NW11 9NN
www.greenhillbooks.com
and
Stackpole Books, 5067 Ritter Road, Mechanicsburg, PA
17055, USA

British Library Cataloguing in Publication Data:

Michulec, Robert
Luftwaffe aces of the Western Front. – (Luftwaffe at war;
19)
1. Germany. Luftwaffe – History 2. Air pilots, Military –
Germany – Biography 3. World War, 1939-1945 –
Campaigns – Western Front. 4. World War, 1939–1945 –
Aerial operations, German
I. Title
940.5'44943'0922

ISBN 1-85367-486-9

*Library of Congress Cataloging-in-Publication Data
available.*

Designed by DAG Publications Ltd
Design by David Gibbons
Layout by Meredith MacArdle
Edited by Peter Rea and Andy Oppenheimer
Printed in Singapore

LUFTWAFFE ACES OF THE WESTERN FRONT

The history of Germany's World War II aces is of great interest to aviation enthusiasts worldwide. This should not be surprising. German aces dominated the European sky from France's Atlantic coast to the river Volga in the Soviet Union. Wherever they appeared, they were lords of the sky for the entire first three years of the war. They overwhelmed the obsolete Polish fighter arm in 1939, quickly eliminated French fighters, and were hardly threatened by Fighter Command in the second half of 1940. For two years they repeatedly wreaked painful losses on British fighters over the English Channel and France. At the opposite end of the Continent *Jagdflieger* eliminated Soviet aircraft in every battle. No fighter force in Europe could survive clashes with the Jagdwaffe. Such a forces only appeared in late 1942 – when the USA, with its modern aircraft and well-trained, daring pilots, joined the war in Africa and Europe.

In the initial period of the war German aces not only flew superior fighter planes, but also flew them more aggressively, using better tactics. In their operation over Poland, the Polish forces were so weak in every aspect of fighter arm organisation that there was nothing the Germans could learn from this battle. Only the war against France in 1940 proved to them without doubt that they had chosen the best route in the latter half of the 1930s, that of building up the Jagdwaffe.

The German fighter arm was so effective that it achieved a 5:1 victory-to-loss ratio, a very impressive record. It is important to stress here that this ratio was not won by a unit, but by the whole force. It can therefore be said that German fighter pilots were five times more effective than their French counterparts.

German fighter methods were learned during dogfights against Britain's Fighter Command, which had displayed inferior fighter tactics and organisation. The battle over British airspace brought into sharp focus each force's differing capabilities, especially as Britain's fighter planes matched up to the Luftwaffe's in many ways. Germany's Me 109 E-4/7 and Britain's Spitfire were the best fighter planes in Europe. The Me 109 E-4/7 was very fast, with excellent diving capabilities and climb rate, and was well armed. The two MG FF cannons could shatter British aircraft to pieces, and provided an opportunity for German aces (other than those pilots with insufficient wing ammo supplies) to overwhelm the enemy with heavier shells and a bigger range of fire.

In 1940 tactics, pilot co-operation and combat organisation were decisive factors in fighter-versus-fighter combat. While combat organisation was badly prepared and executed on both sides, in all other aspects the Germans were better trained. Additionally, German aces were better prepared to explore fighter combat conditions, enabling them to chalk up more victories. For example, Ihlefeld of I(J)/LG 2 claimed 22 kills, Mayer of *JG 53*, 20 victories, and Gerhard Schöpfel of *JG 26*, 17. But no less than 34 were claimed by Walter Oesau, the Luftwaffe's fourth best ace of this period (Helmut Wick claimed 30, Werner Mölders 29, and Adolf Galland, 36). He was only six victories short of joining the 'Big Three'. When the Battle of Britain was over, the best of the rest were Mölders, with his 54 kills for the entire war, and Galland, just behind him with 50, followed by Helmut Wick with 44 kills for the entire war. Later he was able to raise his score to 55 kills, but he died moments after claiming his final victim - his greed for fame and laurels resulting in his death in November 1942. His two biggest rivals had more luck. Each rose through the ranks with about 100 kills on the score, and were never defeated in combat by enemy fighters; Galland survived the war as the Luftwaffe's brightest star. Mölders died in a plane crash in November 1941.

When the Jagdwaffe met Fighter Command one-to-one for the first time over Dunkirk, however, German fighters achieved no more than 4:1 victory-to-loss ratios – losing one aircraft per 55 flights, while the British lost one per 16. While the number of kills was not high, the Germans' tactical superiority was evident. The British also tried a vertical 'wing' formation; however, the RAF still lost about 100 fighters while the Luftwaffe lost exactly the same number, but this included both bombers and fighters.

During this notorious period of success many of the German fighter pilots claimed dozens of kills, building up their scores to enormous levels. At first, however, the German air aces' successes were standard. During the war for France in 1940, for example, the best German, British and French pilots were able to claim a comparable hit rate – 15 to 18 – with Wilhelm Balthasar the only one who amassed 23. Later on, during the Battle of Britain, the situation was much the same. The best German aces claimed about 30 kills – the best RAF aces, 17 to 20. Accumulating all these kills made Germans aces much more effective than their enemies. Until June 1941, when the war against the Soviet Union changed the whole direction of the air war, the few top aces had over 60 victories. This fantastic total was unattainable by Allied pilots; they amassed smaller totals, as they did not add on each set of victories to the previous total from one posting to another.

Later on the score differences between the sides changed even more. All Allied aces ended their combat tours with over 20 kills, while German aces flew an increasing number of missions against more numerous but tactically and technically weaker RAF formations. After one tour they would begin another one, and another one, and again: 200, 300, 400 sorties. Therefore, by mid-1942, many of the best had 70 to 80 kills on their scores, and the opportunity for still more victories. At this time Hans-Joachim Marseille flew against slow Hurricanes and defensively used Kittyhawks, while Josef Priller and Joachim Müncheberg closed in defensive formations against much weaker Spitfire Vs. Their victims fell one after another.

More important, however, was the fact that most of the 'experts' (aces of outstanding ability) were not only courageous fighters well disposed to amassing kills, but were also good pilots and officers who could fly their planes with expertise, and with the proven ability to command formations. Most of the great aces were pilots of this type, but there were also those who were only interested in victories. Consequently, the quality and values of aces and units differed.

A perfect example of this was the *JG 26 Schlageter* with Galland, Priller and Müncheberg, and *JG 2 Richthofen* with its leading 'claimers' of victories - Wick and his followers. From examination of both units' operations in 1941, for example, we learn that *JG 26*'s aces were more effective. The unit had fewer losses and a greater number of hits than *JG 2*, which also claimed many false successes. While it is difficult to explain exactly why such a situation arose, it is possible that the main reason, as is often the case, was the commanding officers. Why, when in late 1940 Wick claimed fictional victories did his equivalent in the other unit not do the same?

Many other experts went a different way. The perfect example of an opposite character to Wick was Joachim Müncheberg: a great pilot, officer and ace. The star of this ace was already bright in 1940, but he reached his peak in 1941, when he led his 7 *Staffel* in the battle over Malta. What this small unit demonstrated through his solitary fight remains amazing to this day. It achieved around 50 victories, half of which being by Müncheberg himself – without a single loss during four months of sorties. The majority of the German claims could be directly linked to given RAF losses suffered over the island: in fact, almost all of Müncheberg's hits are verified by British files.

In this way the Germans built up a legend around aces who shot down far more aircraft than standard aces – up to 100 or even more. In 1940, the *Ritterkreuz* (Knight's Cross) was awarded for 20 victories, but after Barbarossa

the number of victories required was raised to 30, then 40 and finally to 50 victories. For *Eichenlaub* (Oak Leaves) to the *Ritterkreuz*, 40 victories were initially required, but this gradually rose through 60, then 80 and finally 100. By the end of the war, 150 victories were needed for the the addition of *Schwerten* (Swords) to the *Eichenlaub* and *Ritterkreuz*. For the Luftwaffe's top award, *Brillianten* (Diamonds), 200 kills were needed, a figure later raised to 250. These are really only a rough outline of the requirements as the awards given often reflected the conditions under which they were fighting and the quality of their opponents. For example pilots fighting on the Western Front were regularly awarded the *Eichenlaub* for 60-70 victories whereas their counterparts on the Eastern Front needed 100. On examination of results of air combat conducted by the Jagdwaffe, it is clear that this small group of top aces was responsible for all the spectacular German victories. The expert supported by only 'standard' aces won 60 to 75 per cent of all the victories claimed by German fighters. They were the best-trained pilots out of all the German flyers, and arguably of those of other forces. At the beginning of World War II there was no other training programme that could prepare a fighter arm for combat against the Jagdwaffe. The average German fighter pilot flew a maximum of 150 hours before joining a combat unit, where he piloted aircraft that were superior to enemy aircraft. These fighter pilots were led by excellent pilots with great experience, which made the Jagdwaffe a deadly weapon.

This was not to last, however. Once the German experts had won their brilliant duels, the whole Jagdwaffe lost its fight for survival. Only a small proportion of young German aces had the chance to win the *Ritterkreuz* (Knight's cross) and achieve expert status in the West after 1941. This was because the ranks of Jagdwaffe units were filled with young, poorly trained pilots who had no time to gain experience. German aces and experts had no time to train them due to high loss ratios as a result of increasing Allied superiority in the western skies and on the Eastern Front.

The most convincing evidence of this, which arose in the second half of 1942, relates to Marseille's 3 *Staffel* in *I/JG 27*. Almost all this small unit's victories were won by Marseille himself. So, when he was killed, the *Staffel* lost his 'victory machine' and suffered as many losses as claimed kills. In this way it soon became exhausted despite using better equipment than the RAF.

In 1943 American fighter pilots appeared in the European skies who flew better aircraft, were better trained – completing an average of 250 hours before joining combat, while German fighter pilots received only 113 hours' training from late 1940, which later became further limited – and used more aggressive tactics. This changed everything. The German aces were pushed to defensive positions and within one year almost all were completely eliminated. American pilots flew P-47s and P-51s throughout Europe and were as invincible as the Germans had been earlier. American planes were more plentiful and better built and equipped than the Me 109 and Fw 190.

In fact, both these German fighter planes were outclassed by American planes, and not only technically: the USA was by then the attacking side and used their forces effectively. Their strategic bombers flew at over 19,200 ft (6,000 m) altitude, and the top

units operated at over 25,600 ft (8,000 m). It meant that the Jagdwaffe had to enter into combat with them in difficult conditions. The German fighters Me 109 G-6 and Fw 190 A-6 were very efficient aircraft for the middle altitudes, but not for the high ones. When they crossed the barrier of 20,800 ft (6,500 m) they were less manoeuvrable and slower in every kind of combat situation. They were slower at maximum level speed and in climb rates. The American fighters were just the opposite: on exceeding 20,800 ft (6,500 m) the P-47 and P-51 performed ever better. American pilots flew aircraft which, at 22,400-25,600 ft (7000-8000 m), gave them no less than 43.4 mph (70 km/h) over any German aircraft. They were more manoeuvrable and could dive faster.

The US fighters could in such conditions totally destroy every Jagdwaffe unit, including its best pilots, aces and experts. But the Germans had no other option; if they wanted to protect their military industries, they were forced to fight a lost battle. Therefore, from the middle of 1943 on, the Jagdwaffe suffered a rapidly rising loss ratio among their best pilots. The German aces had been ousted as well as the experts. Their losses rose further with the arrival of new American fighter units, which filled the spaces in the sky over Germany. Finally, the German experts were defeated, but not by their American equivalent, however; there was nothing like that in the United States Army Air Forces (USAAF). They were defeated by standard US aces and even pilots; only 25 to 30 per cent of all American kills were claimed by aces.

Franz von Werra, 'The one that got away', in front of a Soviet bomber that he shot down in July 1941, just after returning from America where he had escaped from a British POW camp. The *Ritterkreuz* at his neck was awarded him as early as summer 1940, for eight victories only (altogether 21). In August he led his *I/JG 53* to Holland where he was killed in an aircraft crash on 25 October 1941.

Three images of *Hptm.* Jochen Müncheberg when his fame was at its height. They were published in *Die Wehrmacht* of 8 July 1942, which suggests that they could show the return of *JG 26* pilots from the famous action of 2 June, when they almost exterminated a Canadian fighter squadron. In the photograph above Müncheberg is on the left; on the right is Wilhelm-Ferdinand Galland; the identity of the officer in the centre is unknown.

Left: *Oblt.* Hans-Joachim Marseille in July 1942 (he was promoted *Hptm.* in September). On 3 June he achieved his 75th victory, and on 17 June his 101st victory, which made him the most efficient fighter pilot of the West and brought him the *Eichenlaub* on 6 June and *Schwertern* on 18 June, as well as promotion to command *3/JG 27.* There is no doubt that he was the best German ace at this time. Moreover, he was also the most famous and popular German pilot, who achieved enormous successes in struggles against the British.

Right: An unknown pilot preparing himself for action against the enemy, May 1942. He is wearing one of the few different sets of uniforms and combat flying suits used by the German fighter pilots during the war.

Above: A short conversation between Adolf Hitler and Lützow during a military meeting in a field before the outbreak of World War II. At the beginning of the war Lützow was already an ace (five Spanish kills), a great pilot, and one of the best commanders in the Jagdwaffe. He was one of those pilot-officers who concentrated on leading his unit well, and not on accumulating a large victory score. He started his aviation career very early – in 1931 – so that when he went to Spain he was a very experienced pilot. Lützow achieved all his great successes in *JG 3*: promotion to *Geschwader* command in August 1940, *Ritterkreuz* in September 1940 for 15 victories, and finally his 100th victory and *Schwertern* to the *Ritterkreuz* in September 1941. He spent the following year in Russia, but could not fly missions because Göring forbade him to. Altogether he achieved 105 victories in over 300 missions, becoming one of the very best Luftwaffe aces.

Left: *Lt.* Ernst-Wilhelm Reinert won his fame in the Mediterranean, which explains his suntan in this photograph, taken in October 1943. He claimed more than 60 kills over Africa and Italy, but on 13 August 1943, after claiming three victories, almost drowned when he was forced to ditch in the sea close to the Italian coast (*Die Wehrmacht* magazine).

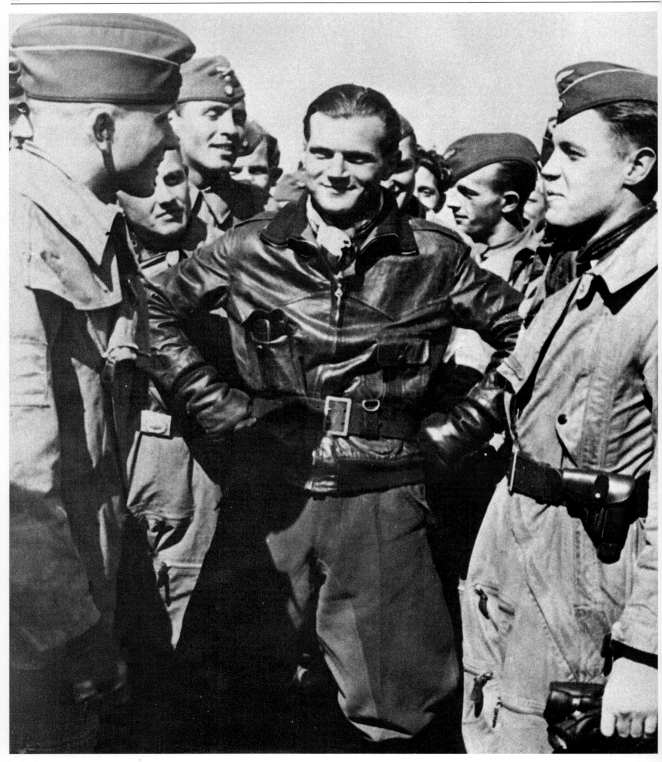

German pilots enjoy their first great success, March 1940. These are pilots of *II/JG 53 'Pik-As'*, who claimed seven victories in one very short combat on 31 March. They attacked a formation of 11 MS.406s of *GC III/7* (a French unit) directly out of the sun, completely surprised their enemies, and won the combat in a single pass. Within seconds Germans shot down in flames five or six planes, and returned to base without loss. There are three of the victors in the photograph: extreme left *Hptm.* Von Maltzahn, commander of the *Gruppe* and the author of one victory in this fight, in the middle, in a dark leather jacket, *Oblt.* Bretnütz, the double victor of this combat, and on the extreme right is probably *Fw.* Kaufmann, who achieved one success.

Above: Karl-Gottfried Nordmann (right) together with a pilot-friend play with a falcon, probably a mascot of the unit in which he served – *I/JG 77*. The photograph was taken in spring 1940, most probably in March, when Nordmann was commander of *3 Staffel* in this *Gruppe*. He was an experienced pilot by then, but still not a fighter ace. He achieved his first victory at the beginning of September 1939 over Poland, the next one was over France, and over England he claimed seven kills, in a long period of combat, however (from July 1940 to July 1941). Altogether, Nordmann claimed 78 victories in over 800 missions, almost all of them in Russia, where he fought until late 1942.

Left: *Oberst* Theodor Osterkamp (pictured here as *Generalmajor*) was one of the oldest Luftwaffe aces at the beginning of World War II. He was born in 1892, so in 1940, when he commanded *JG 51* and received the *Ritterkreuz*, he was 48 years old (the average age for fighter pilots was 20–23 years!). Osterkamp had his first successes leading him to ace status as early as World War I, when he claimed 32 victories. The next six others were claimed in 1940, between early May and early July. He was able to shoot down three of them (two Hurricanes and one Blenheim) in a single combat on 22 May.

Left: The rudder of Me 109E flown in August by *Oblt*. Gerhard Schöpfel of *JG 26*, photographed on 18 August 1940 just after he returned to home-base from what was probably his most famous mission. In this action Schöpfel shot down no fewer than four Hurricanes of 501 Squadron in just four minutes. It was his greatest success, and brought his score up to 12 victories. All of them were claimed in May and August, except one victory of 2 June. Before the end of his career Schöpfel accumulated 45 victories, all of them claimed in battles against the British and Americans.

Right and opposite page, bottom: One of the greatest Jagdwaffe aces of the war against France period, *Hptm.* Werner Mölders and his aircraft Me 109 E-3. Mölders is shown in 1941 with the rank of *Oberst* and wearing the *Eichenlaub* (oakleaves) and *Schwertern* to his *Ritterkreuz* (possibly also *Diamanten* [diamonds] – it is unclear from the photograph). The aircraft is the famous 'Emil' with 15 white victory bars painted on its fin. It seems certain that Mölders won all his victories against the French while piloting this plane, including those claimed before May 1940. 'Vati' ('Daddy') – as his pilots called him – claimed the largest number of victories during the *'Sitzkrieg'* – ten. One of them was not accepted during verification, however. The same happened during May and June. Mölders claimed 15 victories but only 14 of them were accepted. Later on the German ace proved his talent as a fighter, and won laurels as well as great fame in the Third Reich. Before 22 June 1941 he had 68 victories, and later on increased this number to 115 (officially accepted), including 14 over Spain. No fewer than four others of Mölders' claims were disallowed.

Opposite page, top: Berlin, 20 December 1939 – a press conference organised by Dr Dietrich of Goebbels' propaganda ministry on the occasion of a great victory over British bombers achieved by German fighters over the Wilhelmshaven area on 18 December. The German military counted over 50 bombers, and after the fight claimed to have shot down 36. The numbers were exaggerated, but they indicate the scale of the air battle; the Germans naturally wanted to exploit it. The conference was a great success, many foreign journalists arrived to ask questions or to listen to stories told by participants. Seated at the table are pilots who fought in this battle. On the extreme right is *Oblt.* Falck of *I/ZG 76*, third from the right is *Obstlt.* Carl Schumacher, commander of *JG 1*, and third from the left is *Oblt.* J. Steinhoff of *10(N)/JG 26* (behind him in a

civilian suit is Dr Dietrich). Both *Oberleutnants* claimed two victories in the battle, while the commander of the whole formation claimed one.

Opposite page, bottom: In fact, on 18 December German fighters met a formation of 22 Wellington bombers attacking Wilhelmshaven and almost annihilated them. They destroyed 14 bombers; four were very badly damaged, and the remaining four were less badly damaged. One of the destroyed bombers was a Wellington Mk I, N2936, LF-J of 37 Squadron which was shot down into the sea close to the German coast, most probably by *Obstlt.* Schumacher at 14.35. The whole crew led by bomber pilot Sgt. Herbert Ruse was rescued by the Germans and taken prisoner. Here we see Ruse escorted by Luftwaffe soldiers.

Above: Erwin Clausen started his ace career with summer fights over France and England. The first steps of the subsequently well-known expert of *JG 1* were quite difficult, however. Till spring 1941 he claimed only three victories, but was shot down twice. Then, over Yugoslavia, he achieved the next three in one combat only, and subsequently had an excellent career in Russia. He did especially well in summer

1942. In those July and August days he claimed no fewer than 45 victories and raised his score to 102. Altogether Clausen won 114 victories over Russia, and was then transferred to the West, where he increased his score again, this time up to 132 victories. He needed over 550 combat missions to win these successes, and here we see him during preparations for one of them, in August 1940.

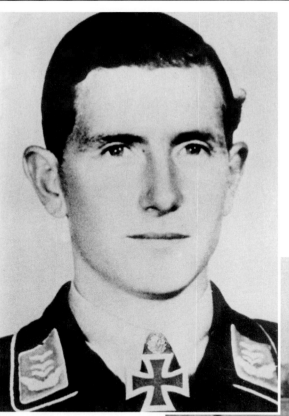

Left: The other of the two greatest heroes of the Jagdwaffe during fights in France in May–June 1940: *Hptm.* Wilhelm Balthasar. During the war against France he was already a very experienced fighter pilot with seven victories achieved in Spain. He commanded *1/JG 1*, one of the best *Staffeln* of the war: the unit claimed 37 victories – 45 per cent of all the *Gruppe* victories. Balthasar himself claimed 23 aircraft shot down, becoming the best ace of the Franco-German war. Altogether, Balthasar claimed 49 victories. He died on 3 July 1941.

Right: After the fall of France Balthasar was transferred to *JG 3*, where he took command of *III Gruppe* in late August 1940. However, a few days later, after claiming his first victory over England, the German ace was wounded and only returned to combat on 23 September. On the same day he claimed two Spitfires shot down with 88mm canon shells and machine-gun rounds. We do not see his last two victories on his aircraft's rudder, however, which means that the photograph was taken just after his return from that victorious mission. There are also 14 markings of aircraft destroyed on the ground (downward-pointing arrows) painted among the air victories.

Above: Balthasar describing his last double victory – two Spitfires shot down on 23 September (25–26 kills). Other photographs of this series indicate that this picture was taken immediately after the German ace returned from the mission, and shows the first moments on the home airfield, when pilots, still excited by combat, narrated events straightaway. To the right of Balthasar we see *Maj.* G. Lützow, the *JG 3* commander, and behind them Balthasar's pilots, commander of *7 Staffel Oblt.* E. Neuerburg (left) and *Oblt.* Troha, commander *9 Staffel.* On the extreme right are Balthasar's staff personnel, including his adjutant.

Below: The next victory ceremony in Balthasar's *III/JG 3* took place on 27 September, when *Oblt.* Eggers received from Balthasar's hands a decoration for his first success, which became the 100th victory of the entire *III/JG 3*. From left to right in the first line: *Oblt.* E. Troha (four victories at this time), *Oblt.* Eggers, *Lt.* F. Beyer (three), *Lt.* A. Reich, *Fw.* H. Springer (two), *Uffz.* J. Keil (five) and *Fw.* E. von Boremski (three).

Four shots of Franz von Werra and his lion cub 'Simba', who for a short time 'served' in *II/JG 3* as a unit pet. (The name 'Simba' was given to the animal after the famous documentary film made by Martin and Osa Johnson, *Simba*. These famous travellers filmed wild animals in Africa for the first time, and their films – especially *Simba* on lions – were popular not only in America, but also in Europe.) Von Werra won his first five victories in France in May and early June 1940. First he shot down a Hurricane of 85 and 79 Squadrons attacking German tanks in the Arras area and then two Breguet 693s of *GB 18*. French aircraft accidentally flew over a German airfield, which alarmed a few pilots of *II/JG 3*, among them von Werra. After a short pursuit he claimed two French assault planes destroyed, and it is confirmed by French sources: of three planes none returned to Cambrais. Finally, on 3 June he claimed an MS. 406, his last victim in France. But the greatest success the German pilot achieved came on 28 August over England, when he claimed that he shot down no fewer than four RAF fighters – one Spitfire and three Hurricanes. Moreover, he attacked planes on the ground and claimed five destroyed. All his claims were accepted in his parent unit although he had no witnesses. It remains unknown, however, how many of them were verified and accepted by the Reichsluftfahrtministerium (RLM). We know now that all his claims about this action (or perhaps all but one) were fictitious, making von Werra one of the greatest liars of all the Jagdwaffe aces. In the photo below are the two letters, 'WE' – the first two letters of the pilot's name.

Right: Werner Mölders' fame increased in the Battle of Britain, when he led his new unit (*JG 51*) in the struggle against Fighter Command. His actions against the British started very badly however – in his very first mission he was skilfully attacked and picked up a few bullets. His 'Emil' was damaged and he was wounded in the leg. Later on Mölders showed his excellent flying abilities and achieved 29 victories, accumulating a score of 54 kills (July–October 1940). Although he was still the best, Galland was at his heels with 36 Battle of Britain victories, which raised his score to 50 kills. This photograph is Mölders' portrait taken at a later award ceremony. Round his neck hangs the *Ritterkreuz* received for combat achievements over France, and the *Eichenlaub* received on 23 September 1940 for 40 victories, which he received from Hitler in Berlin. He also has *Schwertern* (awarded 22 June 1941 for 72 kills). Possibly *Diamanten* too?

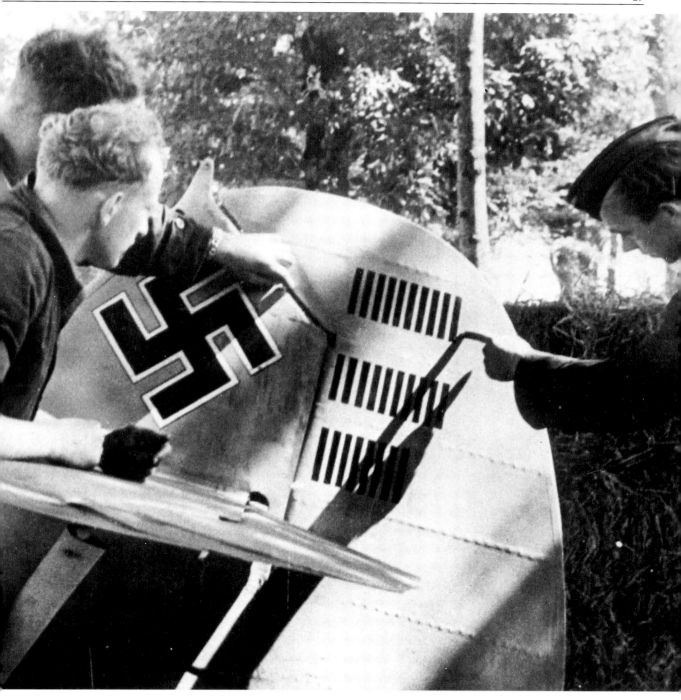

bove and opposite page, bottom: Two shots of the rudder of Me 109E, W.Nr 2804, Mölder's aircraft. They were taken over five-day period. The first photograph shows the rudder marked with 28 victories (the last one was a Spitfire claimed over lkestone), and the second shows 32 victories (three Hurricanes downed over the Folkestone–Dover area). This indicates at the first image was taken on 26-27 August and the second one on 31 August. It is interesting that the rudder is not vered with yellow paint, usually added for quick identification in case of ditching.

Right: Werner Mölders talking to one of his pilots, *Ofw.* Fritz Ströhlein, on the occasion of the *Geschwader*'s great success won on 31 August, when 'Vati's' pilots returned with no fewer than 20 victories, including three claimed by the commander alone. His victims were three Hurricanes which raised his score to 32 kills in just 146 missions. Ströhlein was less lucky – he claimed seven kills only, and was himself killed on 7 September 1940.

Opposite page: Two shots of a fighter pilot group posing with their pets for a photograph after a great success claimed by *II/JG 77* in a demanding day during the Battle of Britain - 13 August 1940. On this day German pilots intercepted a group of 85 Squadron bombers flying to Alborg and annihilated it. Of 12 aircraft the Germans destroyed 11 and claimed 15 victories. On the first photograph are (from left to right) *Oblt.* Jung (commander *5 Staffel*), *Hptm* K. Hentschel (*Gruppe* commander), *Ofw.* Petermann with a pet (three victories in this combat), *Gfer* R. Schmidt (two), *Ofw.* R. Menge with a pet and 'circus' sweater (four) and most probably *Ofw.* E. Sawallisch. In the second picture, again from left to right, are *Oblt.* E. Friedrich (two), *Gefr.* Esser (one), *Gefr.* Brunsmann, *Ofw.* Petermann, *Uffz.* H. Fröse (one), probably *Fw.* F. Blaurock and *Uffz.* E. Isken. As we can see, the best shot in this action was *Ofw.* Menge, who claimed his 10-13 kills within four minutes.

Below: *Oblt.* Josef Priller talks to his pilots of *6/JG 51* which he commanded from 1 October 1939 to 19 November 1940. At this time Priller was already one of the best Jagdwaffe aces with 15 victories, including six claimed over France in May and June. By the middle of October he had added another five, and then, on 19 October, was decorated with the *Ritterkreuz* received by all German aces on claiming the 20th kill. Priller was not only a good shot, but also a good pilot and commander. His *Staffel* lost only three pilots during the whole of the Battle of Britain. In the background we can see Priller's 'Emil' of this period with his personal emblem painted under the cockpit.

Opposite page: Two shots of aces' conversation in *JG 51* during the Battle of Britain, August 1940. In the first photograph are two famous Mölder aces: *Oblt.* Heinz Bär (left, with fingers at his throat) and *Oblt.* Hermann-Friedrich Joppien (on the right in the foreground). In the second photograph are: *Hptm.* D. Pitcairn (in a sweater, commander of *1 Staffel*), Joppien (with his back to the camera) and *Hptm.* Hubert Kroeck (right). Bär's first experiences as a Jagdwaffe ace were very discouraging. Up to the end of 1940 he claimed 11 kills, including eight over England, but he lost no fewer than four duels, and crashed his plane three times. Joppien, on the other hand, was a very successful pilot. He became one of the best Jagdwaffe aces in August and September 1940 when he claimed 25 victories. On 6 August he was promoted to the command of *1 Staffel*, and on 15 September, after claiming his 20th and 21st kills, he was awarded the *Ritterkreuz*.

Above: Another group of *JG 51* pilots discuss combat details after returning from a mission, August 1940. The photograph shows *Oblt.* 'Joschko' Fözö describing his eighth kill (as captioned by the Third Reich press service); the victorious pilot is in the centre. Josef Fözö was one of the best fighter pilots of *JG 51* and was respected as a good officer and commander. He received the command of *4 Staffel* in July 1939 just after returning from Spain, where he claimed three victories in 147 missions. His first World War II victory came on 8 July 1940, and altogether he claimed 27 victories, including 15 between June 1940 and June 1941. He was awarded the *Ritterkreuz* in July 1941, after he claimed his 22nd victory, which was his seventh 'Russian' kill.

Opposite page: Helmut Wick and Hitler pose for a press photograph in front of the main building of Hitler's residence in Berchtesgaden at the end of August 1940. Wick had been promoted to command *3 Staffel* on 1 August, and on 26 August claimed his 21st and 22nd victories, for which he received the *Ritterkreuz*. On 7 September he took command of *I/JG 2*. After this his career was meteoric. In roughly 30 days he claimed 19 kills, including five on 5 October alone, thus winning the *Eichenlaub*.

Right: A portrait of *Hptm.* Wick taken for the German press when he was awarded the *Ritterkreuz*. All awards of *Ritterkreuz* decorations were publicised in military magazines, and all the war heroes had to be photographed for them. Wick is in his *Hauptmann* uniform.

Opposite page: Helmut Wick meeting Hermann Göring, October 1940. During his career the German ace claimed 56 victories, almost all of them in only five months of combat and 168 missions. However, many of his claims were invented or incorrect, especially those of October and November. For example, out of the five victories achieved on 6 November in 13 minutes, three are completely fictional. There are similar problems with other apparent multiple successes – it seems likely that Wick was more 'claimer' than efficient ace, at least during the final weeks of his combat period over England.

Above: Helmut Wick contemplating victory marks on his personal 'victory stick' – a typical piece of almost all German aces' 'equipment'. There are no fewer than 23 chevrons and one bar of unknown significance. The pilot has the *Ritterkreuz* round his neck, which indicates that the photograph was taken after August 1940 – this award was given to him on 27th day of this month.

Right: A national hero, leading German ace *Maj.* Wick, signing a photograph of his Me 109's rudder for a fan. When he notched up his 40th victory, Wick was promoted to *Major* – the youngest officer of this rank in the whole Wehrmacht.

Above: Another meeting of two aces – Hermann Göring and Helmut Wick. Göring was a quite well-known fighter pilot in World War I, with over 20 victories, and he perfectly understood the ambitions of the fighter pilots of 'his' Jagdwaffe. Wick was one of his favourites in the autumn of 1940; he was young, aggressive and very successful, a fine candidate for promotion.

Right: October 1940: 25-year-old *Maj.* Wick with *Ritterkreuz* and *Eichenlaub* photographed at the peak of his career, in October 1940. Only two weeks after receiving the *Eichenlaub* and three days after promotion to M*ajor,* Wick received command of *JG 2 'Richthofen'* fighter unit. That was on 20 October; on 6 November he claimed his 50th victory. Everything ended suddenly on 28 November when he was shot down into the Channel. Most sources claim that his victor was F/L J. C. Dundas of 609 Squadron, but it is more probable that Wick was shot down by P/O E. Marrs.

Opposite page: Two shots of Wick and an *Adler* journalist writing an article for the Luftwaffe weekly magazine. Several articles appeared, but Wick was certainly not the author. All of them were written by a journalist and then attributed to Wick. It is difficult to say who received payment for the job.

Right: One of the greatest aces of the Jagdwaffe – Günther Freiherr von Maltzahn, here as *Major* just after receiving the *Ritterkreuz* for the great successes won by his *Geschwader* during the struggle against England. The award was made on 30 December 1940, a few weeks after he claimed the 500th victory for his unit. 'Henri' – as he was called by friends – was promoted to the command of *JG 53 'Pik-As'* on 10 October, and by the time he received the award he had only 12 victories to his credit. On 24 July 1941 he received the *Eichenlaub*, which was awarded to him for 43 kills.

Opposite page: At last! A 30-year-old Von Maltzahn watching the painting of the *Geschwang* emblem on his engine cover in December 1940, after Göring had given permission for the renewed use of this symbol. After taking command of *JG 53* the German ace achieved only two kills before the end of the year, and then claimed the next four before his unit was moved to the East in June 1941. Altogether von Maltzahn scored 68 victories in 497 missions flown over France, England, Russia and Africa.

Below: *Maj.* von Maltzahn in the cockpit of his 'Emil' photographed in December 1940. There was great rejoicing in *JG 53* – it had claimed its 500th victory. On the pilot's head we see a yellow 'bathing-cap' used to help identify downed pilots who landed in the Channel. Von Maltzahn started his aviation career very early, in 1930, and before 1939 he was a very experienced pilot and commander. His first commanding post was given to him as early as July 1937 – he took command of *6 Staffel* of the future *JG 53*, and two years later was ordered to command a *Gruppe* in the same *Geschwader*.

Opposite page: The perpetrator of the *53 Jagdgeschwader*'s celebrations in November 1940 – *Ofw.* Stefan 'Stefi' Litjens, a pilot of *'Pik-As'* staff. Here we see him climbing out of von Maltzahn's Messerschmitt just after returning from the combat mission which resulted in the claiming of the 500th victory of the unit. The 500th was also the ninth kill of Litjens, who rose during the war to *Experten* status. After claiming his 32nd kill he was awarded the *Ritterkreuz* on 21 June 1943, and then achieved another six air successes. He fought over much of Europe and over Africa. During his war service he was twice wounded, both times in the eyes.

Above: *Hptm.* Heinz Bretnütz leaving the cockpit of his Me 109E, December 1940. He was one of the best pilots of *JG 53*, not only because of his high score, but also because of his flying and commanding abilities. Bretnütz won his *Ritterkreuz* on 22 October 1940 for – as was usual at this time – 20 victories. He claimed the first on 30 September 1939, and most of the rest came during fights against the RAF over the English Channel in the summer and autumn of 1940. The German ace was an excellent shot and a determined fighter, and by 22 June 1941 his score had risen to 34 victories. With the addition of two kills achieved in Spain and another one over Russia, he had 37 victories before suffering a fatal wound in combat on the very first day of the war against the Soviet Union.

Right: A smiling Bretnütz photographed just after receiving the award of the *Ritterkreuz* on 22 October 1940. In comparison with the leading aces of the Jagdwaffe called *Experten*, Bretnütz's score was not great, but it nevertheless placed him in the Jagdwaffe elite. And then, before the date of the award, he claimed 12 balloons, and he proved to be a good commander of *5 Staffel* which he had led into combat since 24 June 1940. Altogether the German ace flew 244 missions, including many over Spain where he spent a combat tour of about six months. Of special interest is his uniform jacket, the sleeves protected with elbow patches – an unusual sight on an officer.

Four images showing the first moments of *JG 53*'s long celebration which took place on 15 November 1940 after claiming the 500th *Geschwader* victory by Litjens. The photographs show all the leading aces of *JG 53* who gathered to welcome and congratulate Litjens when he landed back at base.

Above: A slap on the back. Left to right: *Lt.* Klager, *Ofw.* Litjens (the object of congratulation), *Oblt.* Brändle, *Oblt.* Bretnütz, *Hptm.* Brustellin, *Hptm.* Wilcke (covered), *Lt.* Schmidt and *Oblt.* Götz.

Left: This image shows Litjens thanking Götz for 'hot greetings'. Behind Litjens is Klager, and to the right: Brändle, Götz, Bretnütz, Wilcke with victory stick, and Schmidt.

Above and below: The images show a more demure ensemble photographed for press purposes just after the arrival of *JG 53* commander *Maj.* von Maltzahn. Two unit pets are included. As the press caption claimed, these nine pilots had 112 victories in the middle of November 1940, and had flown 2,008 missions. In both photographs, from left to right: Klager, Brändle, Wilcke, von Maltzahn, Bretnütz, Litjens, Brustellin, Schmidt, and Götz. The aircraft in the background of all these shots is almost certainly the Me 109 E-7 flown by von Maltzahn, used by Litjen on the day this photograph was taken.

Opposite page top: This photograph of Galland's Me 109 E-7 rudder was taken at the same time, and shows his triumphs. All the victory marks were painted in black on a light-blue background and were flagged with the dates of the victories. The rest of the rudder was covered with yellow paint which was removed as new victories appeared. The last three kills, indicated by Galland's mechanic, were won by the German 'expert' on 17 November 1940, when *JG 26* covered Me 110 of *Erp.Gr. 210.* During the fight Galland claimed three Hurricanes of 17 and 257 Squadrons shot down, but in fact he destroyed only one enemy plane. The other two were damaged, including probably the aircraft of P/O P. A. Mortimer, who one minute earlier had shot down the commander of *1 Staffel* and the ace with seven victories, *Oblt.* Eberhard Henrici.

Above: *Maj.* Galland with Dr Dietrich answer questions from foreigner journalists during a press conference organised in Berlin by the Third Reich propaganda ministry on 26 September 1940, when Galland was awarded the *Eichenlaub* by Hitler for 40 victories on 24 September. The press conference took place in a theatre auditorium with a big chart of England, the only place where the Germans were fighting at this time. In autumn 1940 Galland was one of the three most famous fighter pilots of the Third Reich, and his participation in a propaganda show was very much appreciated by the government.

Right: *Maj.* Adolf Galland together with the *Geschwader* dog waiting for orders in one of the *JG 26* bases, December 1940. The German ace is wearing a captured British flying suit, which was very different from the German ones. At this time he had over 50 victories; only Mölders was as effective as he was.

Below: A 'little something' during a meeting of German fighter aces in a forest where a hunt organised by Göring took place in the winter of 1940/41. From left to right: *Hptm.* Schöpfel (22 victories at this time and commander of *III/JG 26*), Carl Vieck, *Obstlt.* Galland (58, Commander of *JG 26*), *Obstlt.* von Maltzahn (13, Commander of *JG 53*), and *Oblt.* Ebersberger (seven, Commander of *4/JG 26*).

Three shots of another great German ace of this period, *Hptm.* Walter Oesau ('Gulle'). They were taken in late November 1940, some time after Oesau took command of *III/JG 3* on 11 November, replacing previous commander *Hptm.* Balthasar, who was promoted to command *JG 2 'Richthofen'*. By this time Oesau had been decorated with the *Ritterkreuz* for 20 victories, the last of which was claimed on 18 August 1940 (he was the fifth German ace with this number of kills). The award came on 20 August, and on 25 August the pilot was promoted to command *III/JG 51*. When 'Gulle' received command of new Gruppe (*III/JG 3*), he had 39 kills on his score, and claimed his 40th on 5 February 1941. On this day Oesau became the fourth German ace to down such a large number of enemy planes (after Galland, Mölders and Wick), and one of very few who won the *Eichenlaub*. Before the beginning of the war with the Soviet Union, he collected 42 Western Front victories, and later on, after returning from Russia with 86 kills, collected another 14 victories. On 26 October 1941 he became the third German ace to claim 100. Note the Me 109E seen in the background on all the photographs. It is the famous 'Emil' W.Nr 1559 previously flown by Balthasar, still with his victories.

Above: Mölders decorating his soldiers at the beginning of January 1941, some time after receiving his own *Eichenlaub* from Hitler on 21 September 1940 for 40 victories. At this time 'Vati' had 69 kills on his score, the last of which he had claimed on 1 December 1940. The next one came on 10 February 1941.

Right: *Oblt.* Erich Rudorffer, pictured here as *Leutnant*, was one of the Jagdwaffe's most brilliant shots, and had no difficulty in achieving multi-successes in single missions. His sharp eyes and flying abilities enabled him to collect no fewer than 20 victories by 21 April 1941, for which he was awarded the *Ritterkreuz*. The first 9 were claimed during the war against France, when he flew as line pilot in *2/JG 2*. By 27 September 1941 he had collected another 27 kills, which raised his tally to 47, and brought him the *Eichenlaub*. But his famous combats came at the turn of 1942 and 1943, when his *Gruppe* of *JG 2* was transferred from France to Tunis. There he claimed up to eight victories in a single day of action, and very quickly raised his score to 72 kills. He later had similar successes on the Eastern Front, and altogether, throughout the whole war, collected 224 victories in over 1,000 missions and only 302 air combats. This means that on average he needed only about 1.3 combats for each victory. This is certainly one of the very best results of World War II.

Below: *Hptm.* Hrabak and *Oblt.* Philipp (in sunglasses) of *JG 54* 'Grünherz' watching re-fuelling of staff Me 109E in Yugoslavia in April 1941. By the end of 1940 both had proved to be excellent fighter pilots. Hrabak led *II Gruppe*, and as the first pilot of the *Geschwader* won the *Ritterkreuz* on 21 October 1940 for 16 victories, including six claimed during fights against France. Later on Hrabak made over 100 kills, all of them in *JG 54* and *JG 52*, and after 1942 as commander of these units. Philipp won his *Ritterkreuz* at the same time as Hrabak did. He was decorated on 22 October for 20 victories, almost half of which were claimed by him before the Battle of Britain. The first kill came over Poland, on 5 September, when the German ace claimed PZL P.24 over Radomsko city (in fact, it was P.11). Before the end of 1940 Philipp had made 23 kills, which made him the best shot in *JG 54*. In 1941, prior to Operation Barbarossa, he achieved another six victories, including two Yugoslavian Messerschmitts. Later Philipp also fought very well over Russia, where he claimed most of his 206 kills; he was killed in October 1943 over Germany by US gunners in a B-17.

Right: *Oblt.* Gustav Rödel was one of the most experienced and accomplished fighter aces of the Jagdwaffe. He flew from the very first day of the war to the last, always with successes, and without wounds. Rödel achieved his first victory as early as 1 September – a Polish PZL fighter shot down over Warsaw. By 22 June 1941, when he was awarded with the *Ritterkreuz* seen in this photograph, he had to his credit 20 kills, collected over France (three), England (ten), and Greece (six). After this date he claimed another 78 kills, all but one British or American. He needed no fewer than 980 sorties to build up his score, which is quite untypical for German fighters who flew almost exclusively over Africa and Western Europe, where the combat conditions were different from those experienced in the East. In April 1943 he took command of *JG 27*, and on 20 June was awarded the *Eichenlaub* for 78 kills.

Above: *Hptm.* Joachim Müncheberg as commander of *7/JG 26* welcomes Carola Höhn, an actress touring the Mediterranean with a theatrical troupe entertaining German troops. In spring 1941 she visited German troops on Sicily, including Müncheberg's *Staffel.* The victories of the *Staffel* over Malta were among the greatest aviation victories in the entire history of military aviation. In four months of independent activity over the Mediterranean his *Staffel* claimed 52 victories of which 25 were personal kills of the *7/JG 26* commander. No fewer than 40 victories were achieved over Malta alone, with no losses to *7 Staffel!* Moreover, the Germans claimed seven additional kills which were not accepted by the RLM, and another five RAF planes were destroyed on ground and sea, all of them by Müncheberg.

Left and above: Two portraits of *Oblt*. Müncheberg taken in May 1941 just after he had been awarded the *Eichenlaub* on 7 May for 43 victories, which made him one of the greatest aces of the Jagdwaffe at this time. Previously, the young fighter pilot had been decorated with the *Ritterkreuz* on 14 September for the standard 20 victories, but not standard was the award procedure. The 20th victory was claimed by Müncheberg just after 17:00, which means that the information about this kill could only be sent to RLM after 18:00 or maybe even 19:00. Despite this, the *Ritterkreuz* was given to him on the same day! The first portrait is a typical picture taken for the 'Der Adler' *Ritterkreuz*-section, while the second one is very untypical.

Above: Two well-known aces of *JG 26 'Schlageter'* describe their combats just after returning from action in autumn 1941. One of them is Klaus Mietusch, on the extreme left, and the other, second from right, is Wilhem-Ferdinand Galland, younger brother of Adolf Galland. Mietusch flew in *JG 26* from the beginning of his fighter career, and ended it in the same unit– on 17 September 1944 he was shot down by enemy fighters. When he died he had accumulated 78 victories, all of them achieved in about 450 missions. The very first successes came during action against Malta in spring 1941, and by 26 March 1944, when he was finally awarded the *Ritterkreuz*, he had 63 of them. The next most coveted decoration, the *Eichenlaub*, was awarded posthumously, in November 1944. On the photo, between 'Wutz' and Mietusch, are pilots of *7 Staffel*: extreme right is *Uffz.* Wagner, *Ogfr.* Müller behind Galland, and the blond-haired boy in the middle is probably *Uffz* Siebert.

Left: *Hptm.* Hans 'Assi' Hahn after receiving the *Eichenlaub* for claiming 40–42 victories on 12 August 1941. Hahn had flown in *JG 2 'Richthofen'* since the beginning of his ace career. He claimed his two first victories on one day – 14 May 1940 – and on 23 September had 20 kills to his credit. The RLM recognised that, and on 24 September awarded him the *Ritterkreuz*. Most of these successes (15) came during the Battle of Britain – in only about two months. Around the middle of November he led his men of *III/JG 2* into a fight to win *JG 2*'s 500th victory. The Germans attacked 602 Squadron over the Isle of Wight and claimed three victories, one of which was Hahn's. After returning to home base, they celebrated this jubilee success, although the attacked British unit had lost only one damaged aircraft. Up to October 1942 'Assi' had amassed 68 victories altogether, mostly Spitfires, and then he started hunting over the Eastern Front, where he was shot down on 21 February 1943 by pilots of *169 IAP* commanded by *Capt.* A. M. Chislov. The Soviets sometimes suggest that Hahn fell victim to Lt. P. A. Grazdaninov; however, this is unproven because most of the details of the combat are unknown.

Lt. Bruno Stolle, another ace of *JG 2 'Richthofen'*, receiving a gift from his mechanic in late 1941. It is a main undercarriage wheel of a Spitfire which was shot down by him in this year; to say which Spitfire exactly would be guesswork, because he claimed 12 victories in this year (three in the previous one), and 11 of them were Spitfires. In the following year Stolle downed his next 16 victims, and in 1943 the last four, which made his final score 35 victories. For 32 of them he was awarded the *Ritterkreuz* on 17 March 1943, and in July was promoted to command of *III/JG 2*. He left it in February 1944 and was occupied with staff work for a few months.

Above: *Hptm.* Müncheberg receiving information from his unit headquarters while at action stations awaiting the order to 'scramble', autumn 1941. He was one of the very best German aces and commanders on the Channel Front at this period. By April 1942 he had had about 65 victories, and as *Hauptmann* had commanded *II/JG 26* since September 1941. His 50th victory was claimed on 29 August, and 60th on 8 December. All his victims downed in about a year's combat over the Channel (between June 1941 and August 1942) were Spitfires – 35 altogether.

Opposite page: Two shots of Müncheberg after returning from a sortie that brought him new victories. These photos were taken around 2 June 1942, when the German press announced the great success of *JG 26* which brought Müncheberg his 80th kill. On 2 June '*Schlageter*' pilots

almost annihilated 403 RCAF Squadron, and claimed eight victories (the Canadians did indeed lose eight Spitfires), seven of which ditched into the sea. Between the beginning of April and late July 1942 Müncheberg claimed over 18 victories, which raised his score to over 80 kills. However, he lost four claims cancelled by the RLM. On 29 April the Germans attacked a Polish Wing and shot down two Spitfires immediately with one damaged somewhat later. They claimed only two victories with a four-minute interval: Müncheberg the first, and Hoffman the second. While Müncheberg thought he had shot down one Polish Spitfire, in fact the Poles lost two. When Hoffman claimed his kill, the Poles had only lost one damaged Spitfire.

Above and below: Two shots taken during a visit to Müncheberg's *II/JG 26* by *Gen.* Sperrle and *Maj.* Hüth in summer 1942. These photographs were taken around 10 June 1942, just after Müncheberg claimed his 75th victory. On 23 July 1942 the pilot was transferred to the Eastern Front to join *JG 51 'Mölders'*, ending his ace career in Western Europe..

Left: A trio of pilots of *JG 53 'Pik-As'* walking from their planes to the rest room on their base somewhere on Sicily, late March 1942. In the middle is a *Ritterkreuz* winner, *Hptm.* Herbert Kaminski, commander of *I Gruppe* in von Maltzahn's *Geschwader.* He was not a typical Jagdwaffe ace, but rather a well-trained pilot with leadership. Before this photograph was taken Kaminski had claimed only five victories and flown about 200 sorties, mainly as a *Zerstörer* pilot. For these achievements he was awarded the *Ritterkreuz* on 6 August 1941. By July 1942, when his unit was sent to Russia, Kaminski had achieved only one air success over Malta. On the right we can see, most probably, *Lt.* Louis, pilot of *JG 53* staff. In the background is an Me 109F with staff chevron, which seems to indicate that it is Kaminski's plane.

Below: Hptm. Josef Priller answers questions from a war correspondent visiting *JG 26* in April 1942, some time after his mechanic had painted on his rudder his 60th victory, achieved on 27 March. In the background we can see part of his Fw 190 with his personal emblem and the double chevron of the *Gruppe* commander. Most of his victims were Spitfires, the main RAF aircraft type downed by German aces during 1941–42.

Above: A trio of leading German aces are welcomed by Hitler at his headquarters in the East Prussian forest, around 25 July 1941. Many German aces were decorated with the *Ritterkreuz* and higher supplement awards personally by Hitler at his offices, a special bonus. Here we have three of them, *Maj.* Lützow, *Maj.* von Maltzahn, and *Hptm.* Priller, who salutes Hitler with the so-called *Deutsches Grüß* - a not too military way of saluting, but customary in Hitler's environment. They received their *Eichenlaub* awards from Hitler at the same time because they earned the prize on almost the same days: Lützow and Priller on 20 July, and von Maltzahn on 24 July (all claimed 40-41 victories).

Opposite page: Two shots of *Obstlt.* Walter Oesau, the commander of *JG 2 'Richthofen'*, taken in summer-autumn 1941, when he achieved his greatest success - his 100th victory, *Schwertern* to the *Ritterkreuz*, as well as a ban on future combat flying that was cancelled in autumn 1942. Despite the ban, Oesau illicitly took part in a few actions, including one on 17 April 1942, when *'Richthofen'* pilots claimed four RAF Lancaster bombers shot down, among them the 1,000th victim of the *Geschwader*. One of these victories was claimed by Oesau himself, who later on, at the turn of 1942 and 1943, and at the turn of 1943 and 1944 as *JG 1* commander, added 17 more air successes,

almost exclusively four-engined American bombers. His last day alive was on 11 May 1944, when he was shot down by enemy fighters in France. 'Gulle' had altogether 130 victories on his score on this day, including 10 won in Spain. This tough and highly gifted fighter pilot needed about 430 sorties, including 130 in Spain, to amass such successes.

Left: Hptm. Gerhard Michalski just after returning from a sortie over Malta in April 1942, standing on his Me 109F's wing, describing his last mission. Michalski was not the top or the fastest scorer of the Jagdwaffe – throughout the whole war he built his score slowly and without spectacular successes. Nevertheless, he rose to join the aces and fighter unit commanders. He collected altogether 63 victories in about 650 missions, and ended the war commanding *JG 4*. He was downed six times, but shot down in combat with enemy fighters only twice. The first time was during his 500th mission flown over the sea in the Malta–Tunis area in 1943. When this photograph was taken Michalski was still without the *Ritterkreuz*, which was given to him for 41 kills on 4 September 1942. Most of these (26) were claimed over Malta.

Right: Obl.. Hans-Joachim Marseille at the acme of his ace career – September 1942. After returning from Germany he was thrown into the battle of El-Alamein, and again showed exceptional fighter capabilities. In this last month of his life he claimed no fewer than 57 victories (in 27 days), and was again decorated, this time with *Brillanten* to his *Ritterkreuz*. For each of his victories Marseille needed an average of 15 rounds of 20 mm, and 45 rounds of 7.9 mm. In this month he achieved his greatest success: on 1 September Marseille claimed 17 kills (105–121), of which about 14 could be confirmed with British documents.

Below: One of Marseille's mounts used during summer fights over the desert in 1942. Hans-Joachim flew Me 109 F/Z models which offered additional power, but also lower engine endurance. From photographic records it seems certain that he flew no fewer than five such planes over a five–six month period prior to his July–August leave. It could mean that he used them without mercy. All of them, as is just visible on the photograph, carried a yellow number 14.

Above: Fighter pilots talk in front of the staff tent of *II/JG 53* on Sicily, early autumn 1942, when *JG 53* was supported by *II/JG 77* in its missions against Malta. Roughly in the middle of the photograph, in light uniforms, we can see two *Ritterkreuz*-winners and top aces, one from each unit. The one on the left is *Hptm*. Michalski, commander of *II/JG 53*; the other one, in the centre of the group, is *Fw.* Reinert, an ace of *JG 77* with over 80 victories on his score at this time. After recovering from wounds received on 23 July in Russia, he returned to front-line service in September, was immediately thrown into combat over Malta, and achieved 16 kills in only his first month. These new victories raised his score to over 100, and he was awarded the *Eichenlaub* on 6 October 1942.

Above: *Obstlt.* von Maltzahn describes his last combat against British fighters over Malta in the middle of November 1942. Among his audience are Italians as well as Germans. His *JG 53* was still at this time the main force involved in struggles against the RAF for Malta. At this time his scoring was far slower than earlier: between early May, when he was shot down into the sea, and the end of 1942 he claimed only four air successes. Later in Tunis came the next four, his last.

Opposite page, top: *Hptm.* Heinz Bär appeared in Tunis in late 1942 as the commander of *I/JG 77*. Here we can see him with a lion cub in the cockpit of his Me 109 G-4 which bears his personal emblem and the standard Luftwaffe European camouflage scheme. In fighting over Tunis Bär claimed 39 kills, which made him one of the most successful German fighters of this campaign. Altogether he collected 65 kills (114–178) over Africa and the Mediterranean, including four over Malta in October, and 2 'Viermots' (four-engined bombers).

Opposite page, bottom: *Hptm.* Bühligen with *Gen.* Seidemann poring over a chart of the new area of operations for his *IV/JG 2* – Tunis, March 1943. His *Gruppe* fought in Africa from the middle of November 1942 until April 1943, and achieved brilliant successes – about 150 victories with minimal losses. The best among the unit's pilots was 'Bühlmann', who in Tunis raised his tally to 69 victories after claiming 40 kills. He twice claimed multi-victories in one day of action (four and five kills); this had happened to him only once before, over Dieppe, where he had claimed four Spitfires shot down. Altogether the German ace claimed 112 victories in 700 sorties, including four-engined bombers of the USAAF. On 2 March 1944 he was awarded the *Eichenlaub* for 96 kills; on 1 May he was promoted to command *JG 2*; and on 7 June he received the *Schwertern*. He was never shot down. Six times he had to make a crash landing or return to base with a damaged aircraft (once by anti-aircraft fire, twice by Viermots' fire) but bullets fired by enemy fighters always missed him.

Below: *Lt.* Ernst-Wilhelm Reinert (left) and *Fw.* Maximilian Volke in front of Marseille's *Kübelwagen* (the German version of a Jeep) in April 1943, the final weeks the Germans spent in Africa. Reinert won his fame in Tunis, where he claimed 51 victories in four months, which made him the most efficient ace of that campaign. His achievements were exceptional because they were won in fights against the Western allies, these being more difficult than the Soviets, whom Reinert had fought against earlier. Nevertheless, Reinert often shot down three aircraft within minutes, and on 13 March claimed as many as six kills in two combats, including four P-39s, within 12 minutes. About a month later (18 April) the German ace claimed his 150th victory – a Spitfire.

Below: *Lt.* Reinert (left) congratulates *Lt.* Zeno Bäumel on his first air victory (a Spitfire), claimed on 30 April 1943, for which he was awarded the Iron Cross II class. During fights in Africa Reinert won no fewer than 14 duels with Spitfires, including three in eight minutes on 1 April. Among his Tunisian successes were four bombers (including a single B-24), the rest being fighters, mainly of American production: P-40s (over 20), P-39s (five), P-38s (three) and one Wildcat.

Below: *Maj.* Joachim Müncheberg portrayed around the turn of September and October 1942, just after receiving the *Schwertern* on 9 September, and being given orders to leave *JG 51* and go to Africa to take command of *JG 77*. There his skills as an ace and as a commander shone again. Within five months of combat service he had claimed 19 kills, raising his score to 135 kills, of which 101 were won in struggles against the Western Allies. On 23 March 1943 Müncheberg shot down his last victim, Capt. T. Sweetland of 52 FG. Passing close to the exploding Spitfire the German ace could not avoid the flames and aircraft fragments, and was killed.

Below: *Oblt.* Werner Schroer (seated) with his pilots reads a chart of the *III/JG 27* area of operations in the Balkans, spring 1943. He was commander of *VIII/JG 27* at this time, and he had achieved over 60 victories. Altogether he claimed no fewer than 114 kills (not counting three won in 1940, which were not accepted by the RLM), almost all of them in fights against the Western Allies. Most of them came in Africa (61), and then over the southern flank of German defence in Europe, including 26 four-engined USAAF bombers. In contrast to other leading aces, his 12 'Eastern' victories came at the end of the war, when he commanded *JG 3* from the middle of February 1945 (he never flew over Russia). The ace career of this pilot started very late, in spring 1941, just after his 23rd birthday. The *Ritterkreuz* was awarded him on 21 October 1942 for 49 kills, and the *Schwertern* for 110 kills on 19 April 1945.

Right: *Lt.* Josef Wurmheller was one of the brightest stars of the Jagdwaffe on the Western Front in 1942 and 1943. 'Sepp's' first spectacular successes came at the beginning of summer 1942, when in four weeks at the turn of May and June he claimed no fewer than 22 Spitfires shot down. Twice he was able to claim four to five victories a day, a very unusual achievement for the Channel front. A yet greater success was claimed by him on 19 August 1942 when, although injured, he joined the battle over Dieppe and claimed seven victories, including four Spitfires and a Blenheim, which were accepted by the RLM. His 'western' victories seem to indicate that downing Spitfires was easier for him than downing Soviet planes.

Below: *Ofw.* Wurmheller in the cockpit of his Fw 190A preparing to take off, late 1942. In the early September of this year he had over 60 victories on his score and was promoted to officer, as well as being awarded the *Eichenlaub* on 13 November 1942. He won the *Ritterkreuz* on 4 September 1941 for 32 kills, including one achieved against the French (prior to May 1940), four against the British during the Battle of Britain, and five in the first half of 1941. Later on came nine 'Eastern' kills (among them eight bombers) and, his best result until then, claims for 13 Spitfires shot down within four weeks of autumn 1941, five of them in a single action.

Above: Commander of *IX/JG 2* (from 1 April 1943), 'Sepp' Wurmheller photographed in front of one of his famous *'Würgers'*, in this case Fw 190 A-6, WNr 550314, yellow 2. (*'Würger'* means 'butcherbird' – the official but little-used name of the Fw 190.) On the rudder we can see victory markings typical for this pilot. They were painted, varying slightly, on all his Fw 190s on both sides of rudders. Here is the version of autumn 1943, with the *Ritterkreuz* and *Eichenlaub*, the number 60 and markings of an additional 18 victories achieved by winter 1943. The most important month of his life was also his last – June 1944: – on 9th he was promoted to command *III/JG 2*; seven days later he claimed his 100th victory; and on 22nd he was dead. Altogether he achieved 102 victories in over 300 missions, and after his death was promoted to *Major* and awarded the *Schwertern*.

Left: *Lt.* Horst Hannig, the famous ace of *JG 54* who collected 90 victories in fights against the Soviets, was killed by the Allies just after arriving in France to fight against the Americans as commander of *2/JG 2* *'Richthofen'*. Altogether he claimed 98 air successes in about 350 missions and was awarded the *Ritterkreuz* and *Eichenlaub*. The first was awarded on 9 May 1942 for 48 kills, and the second posthumously on 3 January 1944. Throughout his almost five months' service in France he won only eight duels, including one on 15 May 1943, when he was shot down by a Spitfire and killed when his parachute failed.

Left: Summer 1943. Josef 'Pips' Priller is pictured in front of his Fw 190 A-6 equipped with a BSK gun-camera (located in the leading edge of the wing, right of the gun barrel). Since 11 January 1943 Priller had been the commander of *JG 26 'Schlageter'*, and this limited his scoring opportunities. Priller claimed his 95th victory in the middle of October 1943 (the last one that year), and the 100th on 15 June next year, which brought him the *Schwertern*. Altogether he collected 101 victories in only 307 missions – therefore an average of only three missions and maybe two combats were needed for one victory. It was a very promising result.

Below: A group of leading Jagdwaffe aces of *Jagdgeschwadern* who had fought against the RAF and the USAAF, photographed during a meeting of officers of different services in Germany. In the first row from left to right are: *Maj.* Josef Priller, commander *JG 26*, *Maj.* Wolfgang Ewald, commander of *III/JG 3,* and *Gen.* Adolf Galland, commander of the Jagdwaffe. In the second row, between Priller and Ewald, is *Maj.* Siegfried Schnell, commander of *9 Staffel* in *JG 2 'Richthofen'*. He received his *Eichenlaub* on 9 July 1941 after claiming three victories (including his 40th) the day earlier (all of them were Spitfires). All pilots in the photograph are *Eichenlaub*-winners (including the unidentified pilot to the right of Schnell), except Ewald, who had the *Ritterkreuz*. He was shot down by the Soviets on 14 July 1943.

Above: Priller was not only a good shot, but also a very skilled pilot and excellent commander. He was cold-blooded in battle and impulsive on the ground. He was never defeated by enemy fighters, which in standard one-to-one combat was highly unusual. This was also due to the superiority of the Me 109 and Fw 190 flown by him over the Channel. Before the end of 1942 Priller raised his tally to 80 victories, so it could be said that in a way he repeated his success of the previous year, when in its last weeks he claimed his 50th victory.

Right: Another great Jagdwaffe ace, *Hptm.* Joachim Kirschner (in sunglasses), chats to friends in his unit about the last combat, autumn 1943. He entered front-line service at the end of 1941, and prior to transferring to Russia he was able to claim only two kills of Spitfires. Only after bitter battles over the Eastern Front did Kirschner win fame. In about 24 months of his ace career he won 188 duels with Soviet and British pilots, and 22 aircraft were claimed as destroyed on the ground. The last 18 victories were achieved in six months in fights against the RAF, mainly over the Balkans, where he commanded *IV/JG 27.* Throughout these two years Kirschner was never shot down himself. Eventually on 17 December 1943 the British caught him in a surprise attack out of the sun and set his Messerschmitt ablaze, forcing him to take to his parachute. He fell into the hands of Yugoslavian partisans who killed him, thus ending a fine career.

Below: This photograph of Kirschner was taken around the end of December 1942, when he was awarded the *Ritterkreuz* for 51 kills. The German ace flew in *II/JG 3* from the beginning of 1942 to the middle of 1943, during which time he collected 170 victories; for 169 of them he was awarded the *Eichenlaub*. Around the same time he was promoted to *Hauptmann*, and somewhat later on left the Soviet Union with *II Gruppe* for Holland. On 18 October 1943 he took command of *IV/JG 27*, and led it for over two months in fights against the RAF over the Balkans.

Left: *Obfw.* Alfred Heckmann started his ace career in February 1940, but the early days were not easy. Flying in *JG 3* he had claimed only three victories before his unit transferred to the Soviet Union in June 1941. He was able to raise his score to 52 victories before the end of 1942, for which he was awarded the *Ritterkreuz* on 17 September. From the beginning of 1943, he flew over Western Europe in *JG 26* and for the last three weeks of the war in the jet-equipped *JV 44*. Here he claimed 15 kills, including his best achievement – four C-47s downed in one sortie on 21 September 1944 in the Arnhem area. Altogether Heckmann collected 71 air successes in no fewer than 600 missions, and he survived the war.

Left and opposite page, top: Two shots of *Oblt.* Anton 'Toni' Hackl visiting a German factory during his convalescent leave in summer 1943, prior to taking command of *III/JG 11*. Hackl was famous at this time for his successes in Southern Russia in the second half of 1942, while flying with *JG 77*. Within a little over two months he had raised his tally to over 50 victories and won the *Eichenlaub* on 6 August (he had received the *Ritterkreuz* on 25 May). He went to Africa with his unit and claimed eight kills of British and American planes, before he was shot down and badly wounded by B-17 gunners. After returning to front-line service he started winning again, and claimed over 30 victories within just over a year of encounters with Americans. Although Hackl was shot down eight times, he accumulated 192 kills in over 1,000 sorties, including 61 RAF and USAAF aircraft, among them 34 'Viermots'. He was so good a shot that he was able to shoot down three B-17s in a single sortie. For 162 of his victories he was awarded the *Schwertern* on 9 July 1944.

Below: A meeting of three great aces of the Jagdwaffe, from left to right: *Obstlt.* Gollob, *Maj.* Fözö and *Maj.* Hartmann Grasser. All were excellent fighter pilots, aces and commanders, and all were involved in staff work by the middle of 1943. Grasser, after winning the *Eichenlaub* for his 103rd victory claimed on 23 March 1943 was removed from front-line service and sent to the staff of *4 Jg.Div.* Most of his kills were made in Russia, but the last 18 were won in fights against Western Allies, including 11 in Tunis. Gollob was involved in various staff work from October 1942, when he claimed his 150th victory and was immediately grounded by Göring. In contrast to Grasser, Gollob never returned to front-line service, however. It was the same with *Maj.* Fözö. After receiving a second serious wound in Russia in May 1942 he never returned to combat flying and did not take up any post until early June 1944 – the command of a training unit for fighters.

Left and below: Two shots of *Hptm.* Jürgen Harder, who was awarded the *Ritterkreuz* on 5 December 1943, when he was staff officer in *II Fl.Kps*. He had 39 kills on his score then, and started collecting the next ones in February 1944, just after returning to front-line service in *7/JG 53*. On 25 April Harder attacked a 'Viermots' formation and shot one of them down and rammed another, winning his 49th and 50th victories and becoming famous in Germany. These photographs were taken to fill gaps in press archives. The photograph below shows Harder together with two other *Ritterkreuz* winners; both were Flak officers, however. On the right is *Hptm.* Prendl and on the left is his adjutant, *Oblt.* Klaiber. Harder was promoted to command *I/JG 53*, and in the middle of January 1945 took command of *JG 11*, where he won the *Eichenlaub* for 64 victories. Among them were 47 RAF and American planes downed by him almost exclusively in the area of the Mediterranean Sea, over Malta, Italy and the Balkans.